The Family Guide to

Dollars, Cents, and Shopping Sense

Family-Friendly Shopping Hacks to Beat Inflation and Maximize Your Budget

Copyright © 2024 by Clair Greenfield

All rights reserved.

ISBN: 9798304139007

No portion of this book may be reproduced in any form without written permission from the publisher or author, except as permitted by U.S. copyright law.

Disclaimer: The information presented is purely to share our experience and for entertainment purposes. The author assumes no legal liability for the accuracy, completeness, or usefulness of any information, apparatus, product, or process disclosed in this book. The author disclaims liability for any damage, mishap, or injury that may occur from engaging in any activities or ideas from this book

Table Of Contents

Chapter 1: Understanding Your Family's Financial Landscape — 4

Chapter 2: Family-Friendly Shopping Hacks to Beat Inflation — 10

Chapter 3: Thrifting Tips for Kids' Clothing and Toys — 15

Chapter 4: Using Coupons and Cashback Apps Effectively — 21

Chapter 5: Seasonal Shopping Strategies for Families — 28

Chapter 6: Smart Grocery Shopping for Large Families — 34

Chapter 7: Teaching Kids About Money Management — 40

Chapter 8: Maintaining Your Savings Momentum — 46

01

Chapter 1: Understanding Your Family's Financial Landscape

Assessing Your Current Budget

The first step to smart shopping and managing your money is taking a good look at your current budget. With prices going up, it's more important than ever to know where your money is going and how you can save. Start by gathering all your financial statements—pay stubs, bills, and bank statements. This will help you see how much you're earning and where you're spending. You might find a few sneaky expenses that can easily be cut. Every dollar adds up, and the more you understand your spending habits, the better you'll be at making decisions that work for you and your family.

Next, break your expenses into two categories: fixed and variable. Fixed costs are things like your rent, mortgage, insurance, or any bills that stay the same each month. Variable costs are things like groceries, entertainment, and clothes, which can change from month to month. This is where you can start making some changes. For families, it's especially important to be careful with spending on things like kids' clothes and toys.

Thrift stores can be a goldmine for finding great deals, helping you save while still making sure your kids have what they need.

Once you've sorted everything, look at where you're spending the most. Are you eating out too often or buying takeout instead of cooking? These little habits add up, but the good news is you can change them. Set a family goal, like saving for a fun trip or a special day out. Not only will this help everyone stick to the budget, but it'll teach kids valuable lessons about saving and spending wisely.

Don't forget about using coupons and cashback apps. With prices on the rise, every little bit helps. Plan your shopping trips around sales and discounts, and set aside time each week to find the best deals. Make it a fun family activity by getting your kids involved in searching for discounts or clipping coupons. It's a great way to teach them important money skills while keeping your budget in check.

Another tip: take advantage of seasonal sales. Plan ahead for big shopping events like holidays or back-to-school time, and make a list of what you really need. Stick to it, and avoid those impulse buys that can mess up your budget. Keep an eye on sales, and use cashback apps to get the best deals. By understanding your budget, noticing your spending habits, and using these smart shopping tricks, you can tackle inflation and keep your family's finances in a great spot.

Setting Realistic Savings Goals

Setting realistic savings goals is key for families facing rising prices. It's easy to get stressed with how quickly things seem to change, but with a little planning and some determination, you can create a savings plan that works for your family. Start by looking at where you're at financially—how much you're earning, what you're spending, and if you have any debts. Knowing this will help you set goals that make sense for your family's needs and dreams.

Start by breaking your goals into smaller, more manageable pieces. Short-term goals could be saving for a fun family vacation or new clothes for the season. Medium-term goals might include paying for kids' activities or saving up for a new appliance. Long-term goals could be things like saving for college or a down payment on a house. Think about what's important to your family and let those values guide your savings plan. It's not just about numbers, but about making life better for everyone.

When setting goals, try to be as specific as possible. Instead of saying "save more money," try something like "save $500 for a summer camping trip by June." This way, you'll know exactly what you're working toward, and it'll be easier to track your progress. You can even use budgeting tools or apps to keep an eye on your savings in real-time and make adjustments if needed. Seeing how close you are to your goal will keep you motivated!

It's also important to stay flexible. Life can be unpredictable, especially with kids! If something unexpected comes up, don't get discouraged. Just take a moment to adjust your goals and timeline. You might need to cut back on some spending or find new ways to save, like using cashback apps or shopping during seasonal sales. There's always a way to keep moving forward!

And don't forget to celebrate your wins along the way. Every time you hit a savings milestone, big or small, take a moment to appreciate all the hard work your family has put in. Maybe plan a fun outing or do something special to recognize your progress. Celebrating these moments helps keep everyone excited about saving and teaches your kids that managing money is something to be proud of. Plus, those small victories add up and make reaching your big goals feel even sweeter!

The Importance of Tracking Expenses

Tracking your expenses is a simple but powerful way for families to save money, especially with prices on the rise. By paying attention to where your money is going, you can spot patterns and find areas to cut back. This helps you make smarter choices with your budget, rather than guessing where all your money went. Once you see exactly how much you're spending on things like groceries, kids' clothes, or entertainment, you can figure out ways to adjust and stretch every dollar further.

One big advantage of tracking your expenses is seeing where you might be overspending. For example, many families are shocked by how much they spend eating out or on impulse buys. When you track these habits, you can set a goal to cut back and use that money for more important things. It can even spark some creative ideas for family activities that are fun and budget-friendly, so you can enjoy time together without going overboard.

Tracking expenses is also a great way to teach kids about money. Involving them in the process helps them learn about budgeting early on. You could set up a simple system where they help sort your spending or create a colorful chart of your family's expenses. This hands-on approach helps them understand the value of money and makes budgeting less of a mystery. Plus, they'll carry these money skills with them into the future!

On top of saving, tracking your spending can make your couponing and cashback efforts even better. When you know where you're spending most, you can plan your shopping trips to take advantage of sales, coupons, or cashback offers. For instance, if you spend a lot on snacks, you can look for deals on those items. It's a smart way to make sure you're saving the most with the coupons and apps you use.

Keeping track of your expenses also helps you plan for seasonal shopping. By looking at your past spending during busy times like back-to-school season or the holidays, you can better predict what you'll need and budget accordingly. Knowing what you spent last year can help you avoid last-minute splurges and keep your shopping in check. With a little extra planning, you can make smarter purchases that match your family's goals and still enjoy the thrill of finding great deals!

02

Chapter 2: Family-Friendly Shopping Hacks to Beat Inflation

Smart Shopping Strategies

Smart shopping is a game-changer for families trying to make their money go further, especially with prices on the rise. With a bit of creativity and planning, you can get everything you need without sacrificing quality or comfort. Smart shopping helps you enjoy the things you love while still sticking to your budget. The first step is to make a shopping list that focuses on what you truly need, but also leave room for a few fun treats now and then.

Thrifting is like a treasure hunt, especially for kids' clothes and toys. Since kids grow so fast, it doesn't make sense to spend a lot on brand-new things they'll only wear a few times. Local thrift stores, consignment shops, and online marketplaces are goldmines for gently used items at a fraction of the price. Make it a family outing—let the kids join in and help find unique clothes or toys that match their style. Not only will you save money, but you'll teach them about reusing, recycling, and the fun of finding something special!

Using coupons and cashback apps is another way to save big. It doesn't take much to plan ahead and do a little research. Before you head out, check online for coupons or look for cashback offers through apps. Many grocery stores and retailers also have loyalty programs with special discounts. Combine these savings with sales or clearance deals, and you can make your budget go even further while getting everything your family needs.

Seasonal shopping is another smart move. As the seasons change, so do the sales. Take advantage of off-season discounts, like buying winter coats in the spring or stocking up on summer toys in the fall. You can also plan your shopping around big sales events, like back-to-school deals or Black Friday, where you'll find major discounts on the things you need. Timing your purchases right means you'll get the most for your money all year long.

Grocery shopping for a big family can feel like a lot, but there are easy ways to make it simpler and save money. Start by planning your meals for the week, focusing on items that are on sale or that you already have at home. Buying in bulk can also save you money, especially on non-perishable items. Be sure to check out the weekly ads from your local store, and don't forget about warehouse clubs for extra discounts. With a little organization, you can make grocery shopping easier and keep your family well-fed without spending a fortune.

Timing Your Purchases

Timing your purchases can make a big difference when it comes to saving money, especially with inflation affecting prices. By understanding when prices tend to go up and down during the year, you can plan your shopping to get the best deals. For example, if you buy summer clothes in late fall or winter, you can save a lot because retailers are clearing out their seasonal stock. This little trick can help stretch your budget without sacrificing the things you need.

Another great way to save is by timing your shopping around big sales events. Holidays, back-to-school seasons, and even Black Friday often offer huge discounts on things your family uses every day. But don't forget about after-season sales! For instance, shopping for holiday decorations right after Christmas can score you amazing deals that save you big money for the next year. Mark your calendar for these events, so you don't miss out on those extra savings!

Grocery shopping is one of the biggest expenses for larger families, but timing your trips can help a lot. Many grocery stores have rotating weekly sales, and knowing these cycles can help you save on everyday essentials. Buying in bulk when prices are lower is also a smart way to keep your pantry stocked without overspending. Pair that with coupons and cashback apps, and you'll see your grocery bill shrink, all while keeping your family healthy and happy.

When it comes to kids' clothes and toys, timing is just as important. Many thrift stores have special sales days where you can find even better deals, and seasonal clearance events are perfect for picking up high-quality, gently used items at a fraction of the cost. Keeping an eye on these sales can help you find stylish clothes and fun toys for your kids without breaking the bank. It's a fun way to hunt for deals while saving a lot of money!

Being flexible with your shopping habits is key to making all of this work. Take a little time each week to check upcoming sales, plan your purchases, and adjust your shopping list based on what's on sale. When you stay organized and ahead of the game, you can save big while still getting everything your family needs. Timing your purchases isn't just smart, it's a fun and exciting way to make your budget go further and help you hit your financial goals!

Leveraging Loyalty Programs

Loyalty programs are like hidden treasures just waiting to be discovered, especially for families trying to stretch their budgets with rising prices. By taking full advantage of these programs, you can save money on the things your family needs and loves. Many stores offer rewards for every purchase you make, so each shopping trip could turn into a chance to rack up savings. From your local grocery store to your favorite clothing shops, loyalty programs can help you save money and get more of what you want.

Start by looking into the loyalty programs at the stores you shop at the most. Lots of places offer free memberships, and the rewards can be great! You can earn points for every dollar you spend, get special discounts, and even enjoy exclusive offers. For families, this can be a huge help, especially when buying kids' clothes, toys, or other essentials. Some programs even offer birthday bonuses or seasonal perks, so keep an eye out for those!

A smart way to save even more is by using loyalty programs alongside coupons and cashback apps. Imagine walking into a store with coupons in your pocket and loyalty points ready to go—you're set to double, or even triple, your savings! For example, if you have a coupon for a snack and can also use your points for a discount, you'll walk out with your cart full and your wallet a bit lighter. Planning ahead and using these programs together is a winning combination.

Another great way to maximize your loyalty rewards is by timing your shopping around sales seasons. Many programs give you bonus points during big shopping periods, like back-to-school or the holidays. If you can match your family's shopping needs with these sales, you'll save even more while stocking up on essentials. This way, you're being proactive and planning your purchases to make the most of your rewards.

Don't forget to get the kids involved, too! Teaching them about saving and budgeting can set them up for good money habits in the future. Let them help you pick stores based on their loyalty rewards, or make it a fun family challenge to see who can collect the most points in a month. It's a fun way to make shopping more exciting while teaching them about smart spending.

With loyalty programs, coupons, and a little planning, you can keep your family's budget on track while still getting the products you love. They're a simple but powerful way to save more and enjoy the things you need, without the stress of overspending.

03

Chapter 3: Thrifting Tips for Kids' Clothing and Toys

Finding the Best Thrift Stores

Thrift shopping is a great way for families to save money, especially when prices are rising. Thrift stores are full of unexpected finds—from clothes to toys to furniture—all at prices that are hard to beat. Plus, shopping at thrift stores teaches kids the value of reusing and recycling, helping them develop good habits for the future. It's a fun way to save and make memories as a family.

To start, look up thrift stores in your area using apps or websites that list them. Many neighborhoods have great spots that might be easy to overlook. Some stores even specialize in family-friendly items, so you can find great deals on kids' clothes and toys. Before heading out, check the store hours and reviews—some may have special sales or promotions on certain days. And don't forget, shopping at stores that support local charities means you're doing good while saving money.

Once you're at the store, having a plan makes the trip easier. There's a lot to look at, so try to focus on the sections that match your shopping list, like kids' clothes or toys. Make it a fun activity by getting the kids involved. Let them help pick out specific items and give them the chance to decide if it's a good deal. This will not only keep them engaged but also teach them how to shop smart and make good choices.

Timing matters when it comes to thrift shopping. Try going during quieter hours or right after the store has restocked. Many thrift stores have regular restocking days, so ask when new items come in so you can snag the best finds. Look out for seasonal sales, too, when stores offer discounts to clear out items for the next season. With a little patience and planning, you'll find great deals that keep your family's wardrobe and toy box fresh without overspending.

And don't forget about coupons and rewards programs! Some thrift stores accept coupons or have loyalty programs that give discounts for frequent shoppers. Combine these with your thrift finds, and you can save even more. Make it a fun challenge with your kids to find the best deals and teach them about budgeting and making smart financial decisions. With a little effort, shopping at thrift stores can be a fun, cost-effective way to get what your family needs!

Tips for Shopping with Kids

Shopping with kids doesn't have to be stressful. With a little planning and a few tricks, you can turn your shopping trips into fun, money-saving experiences. Start by getting your kids involved in the planning process. Talk to them about your budget and what you're hoping to find that day—whether it's clothes at a thrift store or groceries for the week. This helps set clear expectations and gives them a better understanding of how money works. You can even let them help create the shopping list. It's a great way to keep them focused on what you actually need, which helps avoid those impulse buys that can really add up.

Thrifting for kids' clothes and toys is a great way to save money. Before you go, check out local thrift stores and consignment shops, which often have awesome deals on gently used items. Turn it into a fun challenge by seeing who can find the best item for under a certain price. You can also encourage your kids to get creative with outfit ideas or look for toys that might spark their imagination. Shopping this way helps teach them the value of reusing and getting the most for your money, all while saving a lot.

Coupons and cashback apps are like treasure maps that lead you to great deals, and they're perfect for shopping with kids. Teach your kids how to use these tools before you head out. Look for digital coupons or cashback offers for the stores you're visiting. Let your kids help you search for deals on their favorite apps or scan items for discounts while you shop. Not only will you save money, but it's a fun way to show your kids how easy it is to find great deals and build smart money habits.

Shopping by the seasons can also be a great way to save. Show your kids how buying items off-season can really stretch your budget. For example, buying winter coats in the spring or holiday decorations after the holidays can lead to big savings. Make it a fun family game to plan seasonal shopping trips and pick out the best deals at the right time. This not only saves money, but it helps your kids understand the idea of timing when it comes to smart shopping.

Finally, make grocery shopping a fun and educational adventure, especially for large families. Get your kids involved in planning meals and teaching them how to make healthy, budget-friendly choices. You can also explain things like unit prices, why it's important to stick to a list, and how to avoid those tempting snacks at the checkout. Turn shopping into a scavenger hunt, where they get to check off items from the list or find the best deals on their own. It's a great way to bond, save money, and teach your kids some important skills along the way.

Upcycling and DIY Fun

Upcycling and DIY projects aren't just trendy—they're a fun and creative way for families to save money while spending quality time together. With the cost of things going up, it's smart to find ways to stretch your budget, and upcycling is a fantastic solution. Turning old, unused items into something new and useful can help you save money and create one-of-a-kind pieces that show off your family's personality. Whether it's turning an old t-shirt into a tote bag or transforming glass jars into cute storage containers, there are so many ways to get creative—and it's a great bonding experience for everyone.

One of the best things about upcycling is that it doesn't take much to get started. Look around your house for items you no longer use. Maybe there are mismatched socks, an old chair that could use a makeover, or even leftover craft supplies from past projects. These forgotten items can be turned into something amazing with a little imagination and effort. Gather the family for a DIY day where everyone can pitch in with ideas and help bring the project to life. You'll all get a sense of pride from creating something together, and it's a great way to teach your kids the value of being resourceful.

Upcycling isn't just about saving money—it's also a chance to teach your kids important lessons about sustainability and taking care of the environment. Show them how repurposing things instead of throwing them away can help reduce waste and save natural resources. This can be a powerful way to help them think more critically about how much we consume and how we can do our part to protect the planet. Plus, it's a fun and hands-on way for them to learn about eco-friendly habits.

For families with kids, upcycling is also a perfect way to create personalized gifts or decorations for holidays and special occasions. Handmade gifts are thoughtful, meaningful, and budget-friendly. Picture giving a unique photo frame made from recycled materials or a birthday card designed with your own hands. These projects not only encourage creativity and self-expression but also make your celebrations even more special. You don't need to spend a lot to make someone feel loved—it's the thought and effort that count.

Another great idea is to share your upcycling projects with your community. You could host a swap meet or even a DIY workshop at your local community center. These events can bring families together, spark new ideas, and help everyone save money by trading tools, materials, and creative tips. Plus, they're a great way to meet other parents who are going through the same challenges. Embracing upcycling and DIY projects can help your family save money, build lasting memories, and create new skills that will benefit you for years to come.

04

Chapter 4: Using Coupons and Cashback Apps Effectively

The Best Couponing Resources

When it comes to saving money, especially in today's climate of rising inflation, leveraging the right couponing resources can make a significant difference for families. The internet is a treasure trove of tools that can help parents stretch their dollars further. Websites like Coupons.com and RetailMeNot offer a plethora of digital coupons you can print or use online. These platforms regularly update their listings, ensuring that you have access to the latest deals. Additionally, many grocery stores have their own apps that provide exclusive discounts and loyalty rewards, which can add up to substantial savings over time.

Don't overlook the power of couponing apps, which can simplify your savings journey. Apps like Ibotta and Fetch Rewards allow you to earn cashback on purchases by simply scanning your receipts. They often feature specific offers on popular brands, making it easier to save on items your family already buys. Furthermore, combining these cashback offers with regular coupons can lead to double dipping on savings, maximizing your budget even more. These apps are user-friendly, making it easy to earn rewards while on the go.

For families looking to save on clothing and toys, couponing resources extend beyond traditional grocery stores. Websites like Honey and Rakuten enable you to find coupon codes for various retailers, including those specializing in kids' clothing and toys. Moreover, consider checking out social media platforms where many brands share exclusive discounts and flash sales. Joining parenting groups or local community forums can also lead to shared coupon codes and tips from other savvy parents. The more you engage with these communities, the more opportunities you will find to save.

Seasonal shopping is another area where couponing resources shine. Major holidays often bring about a flurry of sales, and with the right strategy, you can stock up on essentials at a fraction of the cost. Websites dedicated to seasonal deals provide insights into the best times to shop for specific items. For instance, buying winter clothing in late February or summer gear in August can yield significant savings. By planning ahead and utilizing coupons during these peak sale times, you can ensure your family is well-equipped for every season without breaking the bank.

Lastly, never underestimate the power of a well-organized coupon binder or digital folder. Keeping track of your coupons ensures you never miss out on potential savings during your shopping trips. Engage the whole family by involving kids in the process; let them help clip coupons or choose which items to buy based on what's on sale. This not only teaches them about budgeting but also makes saving money a fun family activity. With the right resources and a little creativity, couponing can become a game that all parents can win, ensuring your family thrives even amidst rising costs.

Maximizing Cashback Offers

Maximizing cashback offers is a great way to save money, especially when times are tough with rising prices. Every time you shop, you can earn a little bit back, and over time, that adds up. To start, use cashback apps or websites that match your shopping habits. Many of these apps offer special bonuses for new users, so keep an eye out for those extra perks! Once you're set up, make it a habit to check the apps before you shop to make sure you're not missing out on any deals.

Timing is everything when it comes to cashback. Many retailers run special promotions and increase cashback rates during holidays or big sales. So instead of buying things when you need them, plan your shopping around these peak times. For example, back-to-school shopping can be a lot cheaper if you wait for those big sales where cashback offers are higher. Pair those deals with coupons or clearance finds, and you'll see your savings grow even more.

You can also earn cashback on everyday expenses like groceries, gas, and even subscriptions. This doesn't require a credit card! You can use a debit card linked to cashback rewards, or even apps that offer cashback directly for everyday purchases. It's a simple way to save money without worrying about building up debt.

Now, a quick word of caution: It's easy to get tempted by credit card offers promising big cashback rewards. But remember, it's not worth it if it means falling into debt. Credit cards can be sneaky—if you don't pay off your balance right away, the interest charges can quickly wipe out any rewards you've earned. It's important to avoid getting into that cycle. Instead, stick to methods like cashback debit cards or apps that allow you to earn rewards without the risk of interest charges and debt. This way, you can enjoy the savings without the stress of paying off a credit card bill.

When shopping with your kids, make it fun by teaching them how to spot deals and use cashback offers. Turn it into a game to see who can find the best deals or the highest cashback rewards. Not only will they enjoy it, but they'll also learn smart spending habits that will last a lifetime.

Lastly, keep track of your cashback rewards and check in on your progress regularly. Many apps show how much you've earned, helping you spot patterns and tweak your spending habits to maximize savings. With a little planning, cashback offers can help you save without any of the stress or risk of falling into debt. It's an easy way to shop smarter and keep more money in your pocket!

Combining Discounts for Extra Savings

Combining discounts is one of the best ways to stretch your family's budget, especially with rising prices. Picture this: you walk out of the store with a full cart of groceries, clothes for the kids, or even a few new toys, but when you check your receipt, you realize you've spent way less than you expected. It's possible when you know how to stack your discounts! Let's take a look at how to make your money go further by combining deals.

First things first, check out store policies on stacking coupons. Many stores allow you to use multiple coupons on one purchase, and that can add up to some serious savings. For example, if you have a store coupon and a manufacturer's coupon for the same item, using both can lower your total even more. On top of that, you can often combine those coupons with a sale. Keep an eye on store flyers or emails for special promotions, like "buy one, get one free" deals, or limited-time discounts that can be combined with your coupons. Seeing that total drop at checkout is always a win!

Cashback apps are another great way to stretch your budget. Some people think cashback apps only give you tiny returns, but when you combine those with in-store sales or coupons, the savings really start to add up. If you're buying something that's already on sale and you can get cashback on top of it, you're basically getting paid to shop! And if you use a cashback credit card, some purchases can get you even more rewards. It's all about stacking those offers to get the best deal possible.

When it comes to shopping, timing matters. Seasonal sales, like back-to-school or holiday promotions, often come with deep discounts. That's when you can really make the most of combining discounts. For example, if you're shopping for kids' clothes during a seasonal clearance, add any coupons you have to get the price even lower. Being patient and waiting for the right time to buy can help you save even more.

Don't forget about thrift stores and consignment shops either. These can be goldmines for kids' clothes and toys, especially since they grow out of things so quickly. A lot of these items are gently used and in great condition but cost a fraction of what you'd pay at a regular store. Combine these already low prices with any store discounts or loyalty programs, and you'll be amazed at how much you can save. Plus, making a trip to a thrift store can turn into a fun family outing, teaching kids the value of reusing and saving.

By stacking discounts and combining deals, you can make every purchase count without stressing your budget. It's all about being smart, staying organized, and taking advantage of every opportunity. Before you know it, you'll be saving more while getting everything your family needs!

05

Chapter 5: Seasonal Shopping Strategies for Families

Capitalizing on Holiday Sales

Holiday sales are a great opportunity for families to save money while getting everything they need for the season—and beyond. From Black Friday deals to post-Christmas clearances, these sales are a chance to score some fantastic bargains. With a little planning and strategy, you can make sure you're getting the most out of your holiday shopping while staying within your budget.

Start by making a wish list for each family member. Write down what they want and check the prices ahead of time. This will keep you focused when the sales start, helping you avoid impulse buys. It's also a good idea to sign up for newsletters and deal alerts from your favorite stores so you can catch any flash sales or special discounts that pop up unexpectedly.

When the sales start, use coupons to get even bigger savings. Many stores offer digital coupons that you can stack on top of sale prices. For example, if you have a 20% off coupon and there's a 30% off sale, using both will really cut your total. Don't forget about cashback apps, either. These apps reward you for shopping at your go-to stores, adding even more savings to your cart. Even small amounts add up, so it's worth taking the time to check for those extra discounts.

Holiday sales are also perfect for stocking up on kids' clothing and toys. Seasonal items are often marked down, and after the holidays, thrift stores and consignment shops can be full of gently used items. Families donate things they no longer need, so you might find like-new toys and clothes at a fraction of the cost. Plus, shopping this way is a great opportunity to teach your kids about thrifting and making smart choices when it comes to spending.

Don't forget to keep an eye on grocery sales, too. Many stores offer special discounts on holiday staples like baking supplies, snacks, and family meal essentials. If you plan your meals around these sales, you can enjoy all the holiday goodies while saving a bit on your grocery bill.

With a bit of planning and a few simple tricks, holiday sales can be a fun and budget-friendly way to get everything your family needs. So get your list ready, keep an eye out for those deals, and make the most of this shopping season!

Off-Season Shopping Tips

Off-season shopping is a smart way to stretch your family's budget, especially when you plan ahead. By purchasing seasonal items when they're out of season, you can score amazing deals on everything from clothes to toys and household goods. Imagine buying your child's winter coat for next year at a fraction of the price! When stores clear out old inventory to make room for new items, the discounts can be huge. By keeping an eye on clearance racks and sales outside the typical busy seasons, you can keep your budget on track.

A great way to stay organized with off-season shopping is to create a shopping calendar. Mark important sale events, like post-holiday clearances after Christmas or summer sales in August. This helps you plan and ensures you don't miss out on the best deals. Don't forget to check local stores or online retailers for clearance events that don't always line up with holidays. By planning ahead, you'll be able to stock up on items your family will need, at a price that works for you.

When it comes to shopping for kids' clothes and toys, thrifting during the off-season is a great option. Second-hand stores often have big discounts, and during off-season months, you'll find even better deals. You can score lightly used or even new items that other families have donated after their kids outgrew them. Not only will you save money, but you'll also teach your children about sustainability. Turn thrift store visits into family adventures—it can be fun, educational, and rewarding for everyone.

Using coupons and cashback apps can make your off-season shopping even smarter. Before you head out, take a few minutes to search for any relevant discounts or cashback offers. Many stores also have loyalty programs that offer extra savings or rewards. When you combine these tools with off-season shopping, you can rack up even bigger savings. The thrill of finding a great deal and stacking it with a coupon or cashback offer can make shopping feel like a fun challenge for the whole family.

Don't forget about grocery shopping during off-season sales too. Stocking up on non-perishable items during seasonal sales can help reduce your grocery bills each month. For example, you might find pasta, canned goods, or holiday baking supplies at lower prices in the summer. Focus on buying in bulk or planning your meals around seasonal ingredients. This helps save money while making sure your family gets healthy, delicious meals without spending a fortune. By following these off-season shopping tips, you'll make your budget go further and keep your family well-stocked all year long.

Planning Ahead for Special Events

Planning ahead for special events is a great way for families to save money while still making memories. Whether it's a birthday, holiday, or any other celebration, a little foresight can go a long way in cutting costs. Start by marking your calendar and mapping out your plans well in advance. This way, you can take advantage of sales, clearance items, and seasonal discounts, helping you stick to your budget while still having a fantastic time.

For kids' clothing and toys, planning ahead can really pay off. Keep an eye out for gently used items at local thrift stores or online marketplaces. You'll often find hidden gems that are perfect for gifts or party outfits—at a fraction of the price. You could even organize a clothing swap with friends or family. Not only will this refresh your child's wardrobe without spending much, but it's also a great way to connect with others and share resources. This type of strategic shopping allows you to get what you need while keeping costs down.

When planning for events, coupons and cashback apps are lifesavers. If you know you'll need supplies for a party, start collecting coupons ahead of time. Many stores have loyalty programs that reward repeat shoppers with exclusive discounts. Combining these deals with cashback offers can help lower your overall expenses even more. And don't be shy about sharing these tips with friends! Pooling your resources can lead to even bigger savings for everyone involved.

Seasonal shopping can also help you stay ahead of the game. After holidays, look for sales on party supplies that you can stock up on for next year. By purchasing items when they're at their lowest prices, you'll save yourself the stress of last-minute shopping. Make a list of common items you need for special occasions and keep an eye out for deals throughout the year, so when the time comes, you're ready to go.

Don't forget to plan your meals carefully, especially if you're feeding a crowd. Meal planning for special events helps avoid overspending and food waste. If you can, make a festive dish that works as a regular meal, stretching your grocery budget even further. Buying in bulk for non-perishable items or party ingredients will save you money too. Remember, planning ahead is all about reducing stress and making sure your family can enjoy the special moments together. Use these tips to save money, and you'll be able to focus on the fun and joy of the occasion!

06

Chapter 6: Smart Grocery Shopping for Large Families

Meal Planning for Savings

Meal planning is a great way to keep your grocery budget in check while making sure your family enjoys healthy, delicious meals. Taking a little time each week to plan your meals can help you avoid those last-minute trips to the store that often lead to impulse buys. Plus, you can make sure you're using fresh ingredients and creating balanced meals your whole family will love.

Start by looking at what you already have in your pantry and fridge. This helps you avoid buying items you already own and cuts down on food waste. Once you've got that sorted, plan meals that use what you already have, and keep an eye on what's on sale at the store. You can even ask your kids to help pick out a meal or snack for the week. This gives them a chance to get involved and might even get them excited about trying new foods!

Batch cooking is another great trick. On a quiet day, cook larger portions of meals you can reheat later. Things like soups, stews, and casseroles work perfectly for this. Not only will you save time, but you'll also make the most of sales on bulk ingredients. And with meals ready to go, you won't be tempted to order takeout when you're too busy to cook.

Don't forget about coupons and cashback apps! As you plan your weekly menu, check for any coupons or special offers for the items you're buying. Many stores offer cashback for specific products, and combining these with your meal plan means you can treat yourself to better ingredients without overspending. If you find great deals, share them with friends and family to help everyone save a little more.

Lastly, think about what's in season. Seasonal produce is usually cheaper, fresher, and tastier than out-of-season options. Try adding seasonal fruits and veggies to your meals, and explore new recipes that highlight these ingredients. It's a fun way to get creative in the kitchen while sticking to your budget.

Meal planning isn't just about saving money—it can be a fun and creative way to enjoy time together as a family while also eating well. With a little planning, you can turn grocery shopping into a smart, budget-friendly experience!

Bulk Buying Benefits

Buying in bulk is a great way to stretch your family's budget, especially when you need to stock up on everyday items. When you buy in larger quantities, you typically save more per item, which can add up to some serious savings over time. This is especially helpful for families with kids, who tend to go through snacks, toiletries, and household goods pretty quickly. By buying in bulk during sales or promotions, you can avoid running out of these essentials and paying full price when you're in a rush.

One of the best things about bulk buying is that you can stock up on non-perishable items, like canned goods, pasta, rice, and toiletries, which can last for months. Imagine not having to buy toilet paper or pasta for weeks because you've already got a stash. By planning ahead and buying in larger quantities, you'll always have what you need on hand. Plus, when your pantry is stocked, you're less likely to impulse-buy extra things at the store or make last-minute trips that cost more money.

Bulk buying is also a great chance to teach kids how to be smart shoppers. You can show them how to compare prices and look for good deals, helping them understand the value of money. When they're old enough, they'll appreciate these lessons and may even start helping out more with budgeting. Plus, making shopping a family activity builds teamwork and helps everyone understand that being thoughtful with money can make a big difference.

Another perk of bulk buying is that it can help cut down on waste. By avoiding extra trips to the store, you save on gas and reduce the chances of impulse purchases. You can also pick up items with less packaging, like bulk grains or organic products, which is better for the environment. It's a great way to be more sustainable and teach your kids about making eco-friendly choices.

Don't forget to use technology to get even more savings when buying in bulk. Many stores offer loyalty programs, digital coupons, and cashback deals, which can give you extra discounts on your bulk items. Keep an eye out for store promotions, clearance items, or apps that offer additional savings, and you'll have a great strategy to save even more.

With a little planning and a smart approach, bulk buying can really help your family save money and stock up on what you need without all the extra spending. It's a win-win!

Navigating Store Brands vs. Name Brands

Shopping for store brands instead of name brands can be a great way for families to save money without sacrificing quality. When you're out shopping, you might notice that store brands (sometimes called private labels) often cost a lot less than their name-brand counterparts. The best part? Many of these store-brand products are just as good, if not better, than what you're used to buying. Let's dive into how you can make smart choices that benefit both your budget and your family.

The key to finding the right balance between store brands and name brands is to keep an open mind. For a long time, we've been told that name brands are the gold standard, but the difference in quality isn't always as big as we think. Many grocery stores work hard to make sure their store brands measure up to the big names. If you check out the labels and ingredients, you might find that they're very similar, which means you're paying for the same thing at a lower price.

To make this process fun, involve your kids! Take them shopping with you and let them try both store-brand and name-brand versions of their favorite snacks. They might surprise you by liking the store brand better. Not only does this save money, but it can also turn grocery shopping into a fun family activity.

Switching to store brands can make a big difference in your grocery bill, freeing up extra cash for other things your family might need. After you've tried a few store-brand items, create a flexible shopping list that includes both store and name brands, depending on what's on sale or available. Watch out for sales, discounts, and coupons to maximize your savings. You might find that your family loves a new store brand product you never thought to try.

In the end, choosing between store brands and name brands is about being smart and making choices that fit your family's needs. By being open to trying new things and taking a little extra time to compare prices, you can save money and still get the quality your family deserves. With a bit of planning and a willingness to explore, you can turn grocery shopping into a budget-friendly adventure!

07

Chapter 7: Teaching Kids About Money Management

Fun Ways to Teach Budgeting

Teaching kids how to budget doesn't have to be boring—it can actually be an adventure! Turning budgeting into a game is a great way to get the whole family involved and make learning about money fun. Try creating a "Family Budget Challenge." Each family member gets a set amount of play money, and you can assign it to things like food, entertainment, or savings. Have fun with it by setting up challenges like planning a family day out without going over budget or buying groceries while sticking to a certain amount. This way, kids can start to understand the balance between spending and saving.

Another way to teach budgeting is by bringing your kids along during real-life shopping trips. Let them help you compare prices, choose items, and see how your budget holds up. For example, during back-to-school shopping, make it a mission to find the best deals on supplies. Or take them to thrift stores and show them how to find great stuff at a fraction of the cost. These experiences show kids that budgeting is something they can apply in their everyday lives.

You can also make budgeting more interactive by using apps. Many apps let you set up goals and track your spending, and some even have rewards when you stick to your budget. Sit down with your kids and set a family goal together—maybe saving for a vacation or a new game console—and track your progress. It's a great way to work as a team and help them see how budgeting can help you reach your goals.

Don't forget about coupons and cashback apps—they can make shopping feel like a treasure hunt! Next time you're shopping, let your kids help you find the best deals. Create a fun reward system where they get points for every coupon or discount they find, and they can trade those points in for little prizes or treats. This teaches them the value of money while making shopping more exciting.

Lastly, make budgeting a regular family conversation. Set aside some time each week to talk about your finances—what's working, what's not, and how you can save more. Encourage your kids to share their ideas about saving money, and set new goals together. When you hit those goals, celebrate! Whether you saved enough for a family outing or stuck to your budget for a month, take time to enjoy the progress. By keeping money talk open and positive, you're setting your kids up for a future of smart money habits.

Involving Kids in Shopping Decisions

Involving kids in shopping can turn a regular trip into an exciting adventure while teaching them valuable money lessons. When your children help with shopping decisions, they start to understand how money works, how to make smart choices, and how to stick to a budget. It's a great way to teach responsibility in a fun and practical way, and they'll carry those lessons into adulthood.

Start with a simple task like making the shopping list together. Turn it into a fun challenge by asking them to think about what's really needed versus what's just a want. For example, when you're planning meals for the week, have them help choose one or two healthy snacks for the cart. This gives them a chance to feel involved and learn about making healthier choices that also save money.

To make shopping even more exciting, set a budget challenge. Let your kids find the best deals within that budget, using coupons or cash-back apps to get even more savings. They'll love the chance to compete with you to find the best bargains, and you'll be impressed by how much they can learn about comparison shopping, price tags, and smart use of technology.

Thrifting can be another fun way to teach your kids about saving money. Take them to a local thrift store or consignment shop and turn it into a treasure hunt. Challenge them to find a cool outfit or toy that fits their interests while staying within your budget. Not only will they learn to appreciate a good deal, but they'll also understand the value of reusing and recycling, which is great for both your wallet and the planet.

Lastly, turn seasonal shopping into a family project. Talk about upcoming holidays or special events and plan ahead to catch sales, whether it's after the holidays or when things go on clearance. You can teach your kids how to shop smart by looking for off-season deals, and soon they'll understand how planning ahead helps save money in the long run. With each shopping trip, you'll not only be keeping your budget on track but also creating lasting memories while teaching important financial skills.

Encouraging Savings Habits

Teaching your family how to save money can actually be a lot of fun, and it's a great way to build smart habits that'll last a lifetime! It's not just about cutting costs, it's about making saving money feel like an adventure. By talking about money in a way that's open and exciting, you can show your kids how to be wise with their spending without it feeling like a chore.

One awesome way to get everyone involved is by setting a family savings goal. Maybe it's for a trip to the zoo, a family game night, or a new board game you can all play together. Whatever it is, having a goal that everyone can get excited about makes saving feel like a team effort. Use a big chart or a jar to track your progress, and as the money grows, so does the excitement! Every time you hit a milestone, do something fun to celebrate, like adding stickers or having a mini dance party. The more you make it fun, the more your family will be motivated to keep saving!

Thrifting is another way to turn saving into a fun family outing. Who doesn't love a good treasure hunt? Take your kids to a thrift store and challenge them to find the coolest clothes or toys with a set budget. You'll be amazed at the creative, unique things you can find, and it's a great way to teach your kids that you don't have to spend a ton of money to get awesome stuff. You can even make it a competition—whoever finds the best deal wins a silly prize! It's a win-win: you save money, have fun, and teach your kids how to be smart shoppers.

Then, there's couponing and cashback apps—yes, they can actually be exciting! Make it a family game to see who can find the best deal. Have everyone search for coupons or find cashback offers for items on your shopping list. It's like a real-life scavenger hunt, and the reward is saving money. Afterward, head to the store with all your deals and watch how much you can save together. Every time you use a coupon or app, it's like hitting a mini jackpot!

Lastly, let's talk about shopping for seasons. Teach your kids the magic of timing your purchases. For example, when the season's over, that's when the real deals begin! After winter ends, buy those warm coats at a discount for next year. Or, after the holidays, stock up on decorations for the next big occasion. When you show your kids how to plan ahead, they'll start thinking about shopping in a whole new way—and it's a skill they'll use forever.

Saving money doesn't have to be all serious and boring! When you make it fun and include everyone in the process, it turns into an exciting family adventure where everyone wins.

08

Chapter 8: Maintaining Your Savings Momentum

Regularly Reviewing Your Budget

Reviewing your budget regularly is a smart and simple way to stay on top of your finances, especially with prices changing all the time. As parents, it's important to know where your money is going so you can make every dollar work harder for you. Set aside a specific time each month to sit down as a family and go over your budget together. Not only does this help you stay organized, but it's also a great way to teach your kids about money. Involving them makes it more fun and shows them how they can be part of the process too.

While you're looking over your budget, take a close look at where the money is going. Are there areas where you might be overspending? Maybe those spontaneous takeout meals are adding up, or you're picking up extra stuff you didn't plan for. Try to identify one place where you could cut back, and make it a fun family challenge to see if you can save just a little more each month. Maybe one week, everyone skips buying snacks at the store, or the kids help you find the best sales. You'll be surprised how quickly those little changes can add up!

As prices change, your budget might need a little adjusting. Maybe you're spending more on groceries or kids' clothing than you planned. It's a good time to think about those bigger purchases, too—like buying winter coats at the end of the season, or shopping for school supplies in late summer when they're on sale. These simple strategies can keep your family prepared and help you stick to your budget. Plus, planning ahead means you won't be caught off guard by surprise expenses.

Don't forget about all the great ways to save with coupons and cashback apps! During your budget check, take a look at how you're using them. Are you getting the best deals? Explore some new apps or websites that might offer discounts on things you buy often. Sharing your best finds with the family is a fun way to make saving money a team effort. You'll all feel pretty proud when you see how much you can save just by taking a little extra time to look for deals.

And don't forget to celebrate when you hit a savings goal! Whether it's a small win—like finding a great coupon—or saving for something bigger, take a moment to appreciate it. Maybe you have a family movie night or treat everyone to a fun activity with the money you saved. Recognizing your success will keep everyone motivated and excited about continuing to make smart choices with your money.

Regularly reviewing your budget isn't just about cutting back—it's about working together as a family to be more thoughtful with your spending and saving. When you do it with a little enthusiasm, teamwork, and fun, you'll find that managing your money becomes much easier—and even a little exciting!

Celebrating Savings Milestones

Celebrating savings milestones is more than just about the numbers; it's about recognizing the effort your family puts into sticking to a budget and making smart choices. Even when things seem tight, it's important to take a moment to appreciate the progress you've made. Whether you've reached a savings goal, snagged great deals with coupons, or found hidden treasures at a thrift store, each win is worth celebrating! By making a habit of celebrating these moments, you turn saving money from something that feels like a chore into something fun and exciting for everyone.

One fun way to mark your progress is by creating a "savings jar." Whenever you hit a milestone, add a coin, note, or small token to the jar. Watching it fill up over time will give everyone a clear picture of how far you've come. Plus, it makes for a great conversation starter! Gather around the jar and talk about how you got to that point—whether it was finding awesome deals with cashback apps or planning ahead for seasonal sales. Involving your kids in the celebration helps them see that saving money can be rewarding and gives them a sense of pride in their part of the family's financial journey.

Another way to keep the excitement going is by planning rewards for hitting savings goals. For example, when you save a certain amount, treat your family to something special. This could be a trip to the park, a fun dinner out, or even a cozy movie night with homemade popcorn. The goal is to make the reward something everyone enjoys without breaking the bank. By tying rewards to savings, you show your kids that being smart with money can lead to fun experiences, and they'll be more motivated to keep saving!

Involve your kids in setting future savings goals, too. Ask them what they'd like to save for, whether it's a family vacation, a new bike, or just a fun day out. When they get to help choose the goal, they'll be even more excited to save for it. Encourage them to come up with ideas for how to save, like using coupons, finding seasonal sales, or even coming up with creative ways to cut back on small purchases. By making saving money a team effort, you're teaching them important lessons about patience, teamwork, and the rewards of being smart with finances.

Finally, keep track of your savings journey by creating a family savings journal or digital scrapbook. Take photos, write down milestones, and reflect on your successes. This gives you a fun way to look back at how far you've come and reminds everyone how rewarding it can be to make thoughtful financial choices. Plus, when your kids see the impact of their savings, they're more likely to carry these habits into their adult lives.

Celebrating savings milestones is about more than just the money—it's about building a positive, can-do attitude toward managing your family's finances. By making it fun, involving everyone, and rewarding progress along the way, you're helping your family become savvy savers who are ready to take on whatever comes next!

Adapting to Changing Financial Circumstances

With everything changing so fast in the world today, it can feel tricky to keep your family's finances on track. But with a little planning and creativity, you can adapt to the shifts and keep your budget in check without sacrificing the things that matter most. The first step is to take a good look at your finances. Sit down and review how much money is coming in, where it's going, and how much you're saving. Finding areas where you can cut back will give you more control and help you make smarter choices as you navigate changing financial times.

One of the easiest ways to save is by getting creative with your shopping habits. If you've never tried thrifting, now's a great time! Thrift stores are full of gently used kids' clothes, toys, and even household items at a fraction of what you'd pay in a regular store. Not only does this save money, but it also gives you a chance to teach your kids about the value of reusing things. Make it a fun family adventure to visit local thrift shops and see what treasures you can find together. You might be surprised at what gems you can discover!

Another simple way to save is by using coupons and cashback apps. These tools can seriously add up over time, especially on grocery bills and everyday shopping. Take a little time to explore which apps work best for your family and check out couponing communities online for tips and deals. You could even turn it into a game where everyone tries to find the best coupon or deal. Imagine using the money you saved on groceries for a fun family day out or putting it toward something you all really want—it's all about making your money stretch further!

Seasonal shopping can also be a huge money-saver. By timing your purchases around big sales or the end-of-season markdowns, you can score great deals on things like clothing, holiday decorations, and even toys. For example, buy summer clothes when stores clear them out at the end of the season, or pick up decorations after the holidays are over. Keep track of these sale times on a calendar, so you're always ready to snag the best deals when they pop up. It makes saving money feel like a fun treasure hunt!

Finally, when it comes to grocery shopping, a little planning goes a long way, especially if you have a large family. Take a few minutes each week to plan meals and make a shopping list, so you can avoid those last-minute impulse buys. Buying in bulk, especially for things like rice, pasta, and canned goods, can save a lot over time. And don't forget to get your kids involved in the planning! When they help pick out meals and snacks, it not only teaches them about budgeting, but it also makes them more excited about the food you prepare together. Turning grocery shopping into a family activity is a great way to bond while keeping the budget under control.

With these simple strategies, you can stretch your dollars and turn a potentially stressful situation into a fun family project. Saving money isn't just about cutting back—it's about getting creative and making smarter choices together. Your family will not only stay on track financially but also come out of this experience stronger and more connected!

www.ingramcontent.com/pod-product-compliance
Lightning Source LLC
Chambersburg PA
CBHW051218220526
45473CB00003B/1082